The Children's Book of
Cars, Trains,
Boats and Planes

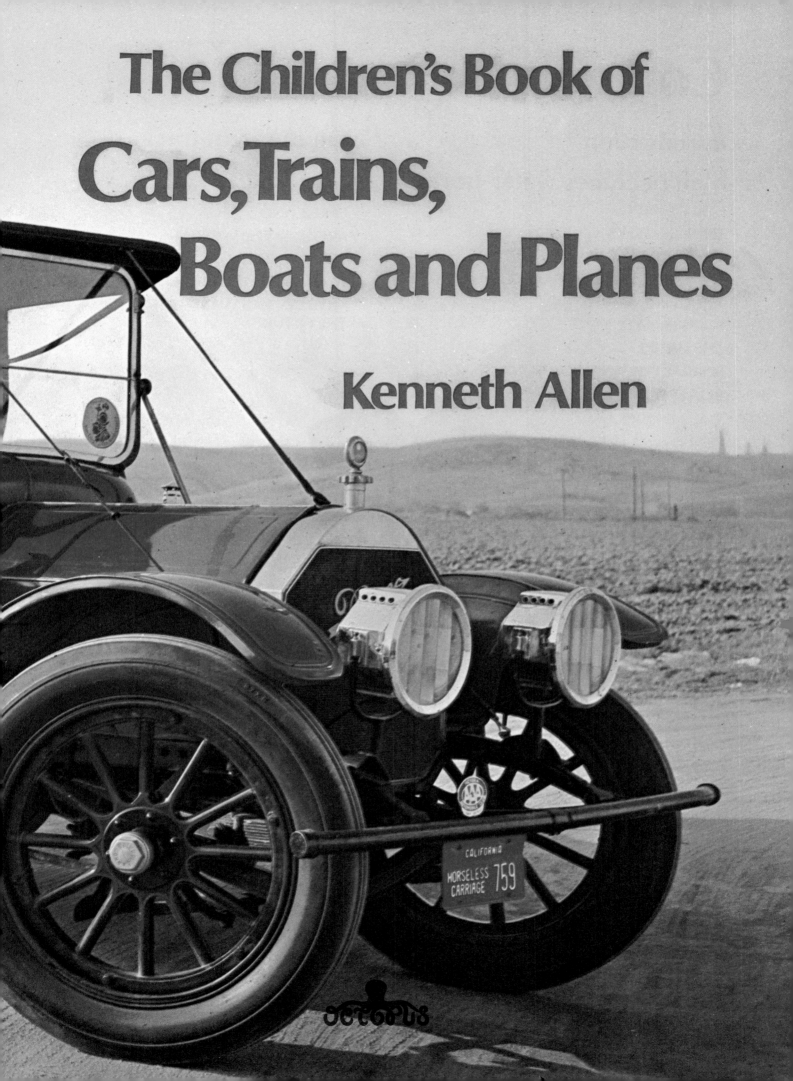

The Children's Book of
Cars, Trains, Boats and Planes

Kenneth Allen

CALIFORNIA
HORSELESS CARRIAGE 759

octopus

Contents

(endpapers): Fishing boats in harbour

(half-title): A 'T' class 2-8-0 of
1903 vintage in Australia

(title spread): 1912 Pierce-Arrow, USA

(contents spread): AV-8A Harrier

Introduction

MAN BECOMES WATER-BORNE

In the beginning – and that's a very long time ago – people moved from place to place on their own two feet. Sometimes they found their path blocked by a stream or river. One day, nobody knows when, one of our ancestors saw a fallen tree floating down a river. He must have thought: 'Will that tree take *my* weight as well?' Lying along the tree, using his arms and legs as paddles, he found it would carry him to the other side.

Later men were not satisfied with just a floating log of wood – they tried other means of water transport. Logs lashed together made a raft; a hollowed-out tree-trunk a canoe; a covering of animal skins a coracle or kayak. And by spreading one of those skins to catch the wind, the sail was born.

The first seafarers in history who travelled great distances were the Phoenicians, traders who sailed from what is now the Lebanon. Later came the Greeks and then the Romans who built their ships larger and larger and rowed them with many oars. When the Romans settled in Britain they built fleets to defend the coasts and when they left, many of their ships went with them. Britain could have done with them for soon the Vikings from Norway and Denmark were attacking the country in their long 'dragon-ships'. We know what they were like for the Vikings were often buried in their ships and many have since been dug up.

Gradually ships were built larger, sails replaced oars and more masts were added. In a three-masted ship, the **Santa Maria,** Columbus discovered America in 1492. Later famous sailing ships were the **Golden Hind** in which Drake sailed round the world; the **Mayflower,** which carried the Pilgrim Fathers to a new life in America and one of the most famous of all, Nelson's **Victory** in which he died at Trafalgar in 1805. This fine ship may

be seen in Portsmouth Dockyard. Another ship which can be visited is the **Cutty Sark.** She lies at Greenwich, a perfect example of the clipper ships of the 19th century.

But a threat to these fine sailing ships was on the way. Steam! The first successful 'steamboat' puffed along the still waters of the North-Clyde Canal in 1801. She soon had a rival, Robert Fulton's **Clermont** which began a regular service between New York and Albany, a distance of 240km (150 miles). Twelve years later the **Savannah,** a sailing ship fitted with engines, made the first crossing of the Atlantic, partly under steam.

From these small, early steamships came the great liners of the 20th century – the **Mauretania, Queen Mary,** the two **Queen Elizabeths, Normandie** and **Bremen.**

Warships, too, have grown steadily larger. In time oil took the place of coal, then diesel and now, today, nuclear power. The world's largest warship is the USS **Enterprise,** an aircraft carrier. She has eight nuclear reactors which drive her 87,057 tonnes, her crew of 4,600 men and 100 aircraft through the water at 35 knots nearly 64km (40 miles) an hour.

ON THE RIGHT TRACKS

There is really nothing new about the railway, at least, about the track itself. In ancient Greece heavy carts ran along tracks formed by deep ruts in the roads of the time. This kind of 'track' returned in the Middle Ages, but instead of ruts, men began to lay down wooden lines over which wheeled carts could carry coal from the mines. Empty wagons were hauled to the pithead by a horse, loaded, then allowed to run downhill by gravity. This was to prove the ancestor of the modern railway.

The first man to develop a steam engine running upon a track was a Cornishman, Robert Trevithick. In 1804, 'Cap'n Dick', as he was called, built the world's first successful steam engine and later showed off another. Named **Catch Me Who Can** it ran in London on a circular track.

The best known of these early pioneers was George Stephenson. He could not even write his name until he was 19 but he proved to be a first-class engineer, inventing an engine that drew eight loaded coal wagons. He named it **Blücher.**

His great chance came when some mine-owners decided to build a railway line between Stockton and Darlington. There was a contest to find the best engine. Five were entered but Stephenson's **Locomotion** was by far the best. Other countries began to build railways and soon some fine locomotives were pulling some very comfortable coaches.

Nowhere were the advantages of rail travel more obvious than in the USA and Canada. Huge distances seemed shortened by the steam railway which offered much more comfortable and convenient travel than the horse or covered wagon.

Back in Britain, the various local railways had become joined into the 'Big Four'; the Southern (SR), Great Western (GWR), London and North Eastern (LNER) and the London Midland and Scottish (LMS). Each company tried to outdo the others, both for comfort, timing and speed. The final speed victory for a steam-driven locomotive went to the LNER whose streamlined **Mallard** reached the speed of 201km/hr (126 mph).

But slowly the Golden Age of steam trains was coming to an end. In 1948 the four great British companies were joined as one under a single name – British Rail. By then steam had given way to diesel. Today, gas turbine engines have come into use together, of course, with electricity. Indeed, most of Britain's main lines are now completely electrified.

Further developments include the British Rail Advanced Passenger Train (APT) which can do a maximum speed of 200km/hr (125mph).

HORSELESS CARRIAGES

There would be no fast gleaming motor-cars today had not someone, long ago, invented the wheel. This was probably done by cutting sections off a tree-trunk, fixing them on spindles and attaching them to a wooden frame. In time this became the chariot.

In Tudor times there were long 'wains', or wagons which in time gave way to stage coaches, Soon, large numbers of different vehicles were using the roads but all were drawn by horses. Yet, in the 13th century, an English scholar named Roger Bacon had written: 'We shall be able to propel carriages with incredible speed without the aid of any animal.'

The first man to make these words come true was Nicholas Cugnot, a Frenchman. He fixed a large copper boiler onto three wheels and tried it out in the streets of Paris in 1770. With a hiss of steam it began to move, then ran into a brick wall and overturned!

Some 14 years later, in England, an engineer named William Murdoch made a model of a steam-carriage. It worked well but he never built a full-sized car. But one of his pupils, Robert Trevithick or 'Cap'n Dick', saw what could be done. He built the first full-size steam-carriage ever seen in England. Others followed and soon steam-driven carriages and coaches were travelling at more than 32km (20 miles) an hour. But it was this very speed that made many people call for them to be taken off English roads. Parliament then ordered that a man should walk in front of every steam-driven vehicle, with a red warning flag.

Meanwhile, France and Germany had both made a number of steam-driven vehicles, but a new type of engine was sought. The first man to succeed in this was a German, Karl Benz. His first car, in 1885, was driven, not by steam but by petrol. At the same time another German, Gottlieb Daimler, was working on a similar car which took to the road in 1886. Others followed and two Frenchmen, René Panhard and Emile Levassor, changed the general design of cars. Earlier ones looked like horse-drawn carriages with an engine in the middle. They took the engine from beneath the driver's seat and placed it under a hood at the front. Thus cars lost that 'horseless-carriage' look.

Other types of cars were also to be seen on the road. Some were driven by electricity which proved quieter and cleaner than the petrol engine. Few were to be seen in the 20th century, however. The steam-driven car had a longer life. An American

version, the **Stanley Steamer,** was still seen in the USA in the 1920s.

Mass production, meant that prices tumbled. Very soon cars were within reach of many people. The motoring age had arrived!

There are still people who prefer to travel under their own power. Such people – and they are of all ages – use the bicycle. The first 'bicycle' was called the Hobby-horse. It had no pedals; the rider pushed himself along with his feet. When pedals were added, someone tried making the front wheel large and the rear wheel small. This gave it the name of 'Penny-farthing', from copper coins of the time. Next came the safety bicycle similar to the one we know today. At about the same time bicycles were becoming more popular, the internal combustion engine was also being developed. Again it was Karl Benz and Gottlieb Daimler who independently combined the two into early models of the powerful motor-cycle we know today.

INTO THE SKY

From the dawn of history people have looked into the sky and watched, with envy, as birds soared and swooped above them. Many tried to copy them and some amazing machines were invented. None succeeded, however. By the beginning of the 18th century, people were trying out hot-air balloons. As hot air is lighter than cold, a bag with heated air will rise, taking the bag and people, perhaps, with it. Two Frenchmen, the Montgolfier brothers, made such a balloon, and a friend, Pilâtre de Rozier, went up in it to a height of 25.6m (84ft). He went no higher for the balloon was firmly held by a rope of that length fixed to the ground.

This attempt caused such a sensation that the following month – November 1783 – the balloon rose again. This time it carried two men in a wicker basket. It rose to 915m (3,000ft), sailed over Paris and came down 8km (5 miles) from its starting point.

Two years later Jean-Pierre Blanchard and an American, John Jeffries, drifted across the English Channel. Yet although balloons could raise people from the ground, they still could not fly. The pilot could not go where he wished but where the winds blew him. The first solution came in 1884 when an airship, **La France,** flew on a controlled course at 24km/hr (15mph). It was powered by a small electric motor.

But people were still searching for a 'heavier-than-air' machine. The leader in this field was a German, Otto Lilienthal. He built several gliders, making 2,000 successful flights, then, as he was about to place a small engine in one of them, he fell from a height of 15m (50ft) and died soon afterwards.

His work inspired others. Two young American brothers, Orville and Wilbur Wright made the world's first flight in a heavier-than-air machine. This was from the windswept sands of Kitty Hawk in North Carolina, USA, on 17 December 1903. The machine was made of canvas-covered wood . . . but it flew.

Others soon followed. Alberto Santos-Dumont, for example, made the first public aeroplane flight in Europe in 1908. A year later, Louis Blériot made the first crossing of the English Channel, landing at Dover. And so Europeans and Americans began to build and fly aeroplanes. For the most part these machines were built in very small numbers and usually by the men who were to fly them. Then came August 1914 and World War I. Now the making of aircraft became the concern of governments, not of enthusiasts. Great Britain, for example, went to war with 154 aeroplanes. By the end of the war, four years later, 55,000 had come from her factories.

When the war ended, many countries found themselves with trained pilots and large numbers of machines that could carry passengers and cargo. Then, in 1919, two English pilots, John Alcock and Arthur Whitten-Brown flew non-stop across the Atlantic Ocean. Suddenly, it seemed, the world was shrinking. Journeys that had taken days or weeks, now only took hours.

During the next 20 years many pilots set out to blaze new trails across the skies of the world. Then came World War II in 1939. Once again, war gave a great boost to flying.

After the war ended in 1945 important lessons which had been learned were put to good use in the years ahead. The newer and better aircraft that had been built and the great airports that lay waiting to be used, changed civilian flying. More and more people began to take to the air, designs and performances of aircraft steadily improved.

The world's latest commercial aeroplane is the result of a partnership between Britain and France . . . the **Concorde.** This machine has already cut flying time in half, crossing the Atlantic in little more than three hours.

Having looked briefly at the amazing world of transport, let us think again of what has happened in that world during the last 100 years. The great liners and warships are now driven by diesel and nuclear power; steam has disappeared on the railways, diesel power and electricity have taken its place; the first petrol-driven 'horseless carriage' took to the road in 1885; the Wright brothers flew in a heavier-than-air machine in 1903. And then in 1961 a man flew in space – something that would have been thought impossible 100 years ago.

Yes, more has happened in the world of transport in the past century than during the previous 5,000. What will the next century bring?

Man becomes water-borne

EARLY CRAFT

The earliest people we definitely know were sailors were the ancient Egyptians. They gathered papyrus reeds and tied them together to form rafts. Although they rarely left the calm waters of the Nile, their rafts were seaworthy. Centuries later, a Norwegian, Thor Heyerdahl, copied one and nearly sailed it across the Atlantic before it broke up. It was called **Ra,** (*right*).

Slowly, as civilization developed, so designs of ships improved. The clear details of **Noah's Ark** in the Bible prove that shipbuilding in the ancient world was of a high standard. We can also see wall paintings in Egyptian tombs which show that their ships, although large, were built of short, narrow planks because there are no big trees in Egypt. By 1500 BC, for longer sea voyages, the Egyptians made boats of cedar brought from the Lebanon.

It is possible, however, that the first nation to build large sailing ships were the Chinese, for they were in advance of the Western world in many ways. Their large, square-sailed junks can still be seen in Chinese waters and have changed little from 4,000 years ago. This is true of many other boats. The attractive Moro outrigger (*below*) has remained unchanged for centuries. The same may be said of the dug-out canoes of New Guinea, and the Eskimo's kayaks.

THE EXPLORERS

The people of Phoenicia, those great traders, were also great explorers. They were the first seamen to take their ships out of the Mediterranean and into the English Channel. The first to do so saw a great land mass looming ahead. As it was seen at dusk they called it after the Phoenician name for sunset . . . Europe.

Hundreds of years later came the men of Norway and Denmark – the 'sea-rovers' or Vikings. Long ago a Roman poet wrote 'The sea is their school of war and the storm their friend.' In the 9th century one of their long, slim ships, rowed by 16 oarsmen a side and with a single mast, discovered an unknown land. Its discoverer called it Iceland, a name it still bears. Another Viking, Erik the Red, was banished from this same island and sailed off in search of new lands. In 1000 AD he and his men are said to have gone ashore on the coast of Newfoundland, North America.

So this Viking may have actually

discovered America nearly 500 years before Christopher Columbus, whose flagship, the **Santa Maria,** is shown in the woodcut (*above*).

In the 15th century courageous seamen began to explore the sea lanes of the world. A nobleman who gave men of his country much help in such attempts was Prince Henry of Portugal. With small, three-masted ships, Prince Henry sent men to explore the coast of Africa. Two of his men became very famous, One, Bartholomew Dias, was the first to round the Cape of Good Hope in 1488; the other, Vasco da Gama, actually reached India some ten years later. Also, in 1492, Columbus sailed from Spain in the **Santa Maria.** With her sailed two smaller ships, the **Nina** and the **Pinta.** John Cabot sailed from England to Newfoundland in 1497. Between 1577 and 1580, Francis Drake in the **Golden Hind** became the first Englishman to sail around the world. The age

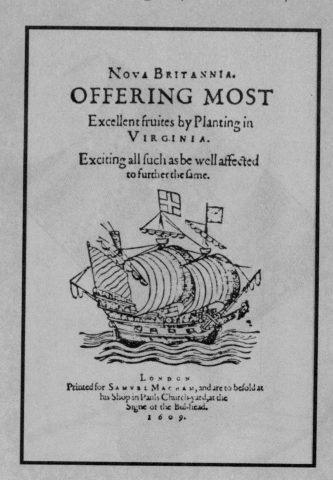

of the explorers continued. The famous **Mayflower** sailed to America in 1620 but 11 years earlier such ships as the **Nova Britannia** (*far left*) were trading with Virginia.

As America had become more familiar in the 16th century, so in the 17th the continent of Australia attracted explorers. They took their ships around the giant island, notably Captain Hartog who had an island named after him, Abel Tasman who discovered Tasmania and the great Captain Cook who discovered New Zealand, the Sandwich Islands and large parts of Australia. During the late 19th and early 20th centuries, men began to explore the Polar regions: Nansen in the **Fram,** Robert Peary who reached the North Pole in 1909 and Roald Amundsen who went to the South Pole in 1911, beating Captain Robert Scott in the **Terra Nova** by only a few days. A former ship of Captain Scott, the **Discovery,** is shown (*below*) and can be seen moored in the Thames in London, not far from the Houses of Parliament.

THE TRADERS

The earliest of all sea trading peoples were probably the people of Crete. Their island had so many people living upon it that it was vital they exported the products of their craftsmen in order to buy grain and other raw products. Their crafts included delicate vases and goblets, beautiful bronze swords and daggers, jewellery and cloth. But a great earthquake about 1450 BC destroyed most of their cities and their trade passed to the Phoenicians. These great seamen sailed from their ports of Tyre and Sidon, making settlements on the islands of Rhodes and Cyprus. Then, as their ships improved, they sailed to Greece, Italy, Sicily and Sardinia, building cities and starting colonies as they went. They also began to trade with Britain. They were followed by the Greeks and Romans. The Roman grain ships, for example, carried passengers as well as cargo. On such a ship St Paul was shipwrecked while on his way to Rome . . . and death. During the time of the great Roman Empire, the world was mainly at peace and trading was quite considerable. During the 7th century AD the Arabs began to take over this trade, and their ships also carried thousands of pilgrims to Mecca. They also sent their ships to India, China, Sri Lanka and Sumatra. Many centuries later the ports of Venice and Genoa became the richest in Europe. Then, in 1492 the last Muslim stronghold in Europe surrendered to the Crowns of Castile and Aragon and Columbus discovered America. Suddenly there were new worlds to conquer. At first this New World was shared between Spain and Portugal, but other nations made sure that this state of affairs did not last for long. And so, over the years, new countries were discovered until by the beginning of this century, the whole world was bound together by trade.

Marseilles harbour in 1754 (*below*) and a merchant ship of the 17th century (*opposite*).

THE GREAT DAYS OF SAIL

The beautiful vessels that were to become known as Clipper ships really came into being because of the American War of Independence of 1776. Powerful British warships began to patrol the American coast and the shipyards of Baltimore began building small and fast ships that would outsail them. They were known as Baltimore packets and were the fastest ships yet seen at sea.

The Revolution ended in 1783 and the USA had to build up her trade with other nations. But trade with China and the Far East was the monopoly of Britain's East India Company. Their merchantmen were rather like bulky battleships in appearance, slow and sure. They had no need for speed for Britain's trade was protected by her Navigation Acts. But America resented this monopoly and decided to build ships that were long and narrow, with soaring masts covered with as many as 26 white sails. A model was built by John Griffith, a New York naval architect. In 1843 the Opium War meant China was forced to open five harbours to trade. Other nations could now trade into these ports, an opportunity too good to miss. Griffith was asked to build a full-size ship based on his model.

As many of the workmen building her were Dutch they gave her the name *kleeper* – 'fast horse'. From this came the familiar word – 'clipper'. In 1845, **Rainbow** was launched and raced to China and back in seven months. In 1849 Britain abolished her Navigation Acts, opening all her ports to foreign ships. An early American clipper, the **Oriental,** sailed from China and landed her cargo of tea in London in 97 days. British ships lagged far behind. Britain replied with a new type of fast ship, the **Blackwall** frigate, so named because many were built at Blackwall on the Thames. One such ship, the **Anglesey,** is shown (*below*). (*opposite*) The most famous of all British clippers, the **Cutty Sark,** one of the last and fastest of the clippers, in her dry-dock at Greenwich.

As the **Oriental** lay dry-docked in London a surveyor copied her lines. The result, Britain's first clipper, **Challenger.** But a new designer, David Mackay of Boston was engaged to design other British clippers. One of these, **Lightning,** was unbeaten by steamships for years. Mackay's famous clipper, **Flying Cloud,** is seen (*above*). Soon British and American clippers were racing home from China with tea as the new season's crop always brought better prices. Then in 1861 the American Civil War began, her clippers sailed home, and the tea trade routes were left open to the British.

In 1865 the Civil War ended. The following year, 16 clippers, loaded with new season's tea left Foochow in China and raced home to be the first to unload in London docks. After three months at sea the **Taeping** docked first, **Ariel** 20 minutes later, **Serica** arrived on the same tide and **Fiery Cross** and **Taitsing** the following day. A great race, indeed. The sea trade was virtually doomed when the Suez Canal opened in 1869, for now steamers could beat the sailing ships to China by this short cut. The tea clippers had to change their trade – to wool. Now, instead of China they sailed to Australia, on the wool run. **Thermopylae,** a British clipper sailed from London to Melbourne in less than 64 days, a record. But she soon had a new rival – the **Cutty Sark,** a magnificent Scottish built clipper ship. In 1885 she sailed from Sydney, survived a violent gale and reached the Channel in a record 67 days. The **Thermopylae,** which had sailed at the same time was a week behind. But steamers were becoming faster and more efficient. Slowly the clippers went one by one. The golden days of sail had ended. (*Above*) the British **Scawfell** and, (*below*) the American clipper **Oriental.**

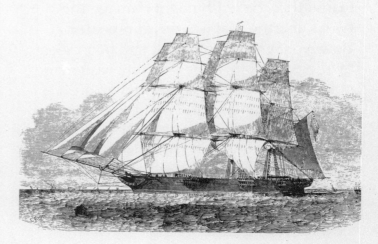

THE COMING OF STEAM

In 1787, a Scottish banker named Patrick Miller built a paddle-boat which he fitted with a steam engine invented by William Symington. Both this vessel and others were successful but he did not bother to go on with his experiments. It was not until 1801 that Symington was again asked to supply a steam engine that would drive a boat. This time his patron was Lord Dundas and the resulting vessel, the **Charlotte Dundas,** named after the lord's daughter, was tried out successfully towing two 70-tonne barges in March 1802. But the canal authorities feared that the wash might damage the banks and the trial was never repeated. However Symington's work had been seen by the American, Robert Fulton, who made notes and sketches. He ordered a British made steam engine and on his return to America, he built America's first steamship, the **Clermont.** By 1807 she was plying for trade on the Hudson River. She was followed by Henry Bell's **Comet** on the Clyde, Scotland, in 1812. She was the first successful steamboat in Europe.

In May 1818, the first steamship crossed the Atlantic Ocean, taking 25 days. She was the **Savannah** (*opposite*) of 350 tonnes. She was really a sailing ship fitted with paddle-wheels, her engines being used for 80 hours out of the twenty-five-day voyage. The first all-steam crossing of the Atlantic was made in 1827 by a Dutch owned, British built ship the **Curaçao.** The first all-British steamer to make the Atlantic crossing was the **Sirius** of 703 tonnes which crossed in 19 days. Really a small cross-Channel boat, the **Sirius** made its historic journey in 1838. A few hours later the **Great Western** of 1,340 tonnes also arrived in New York although she had left England three days after the other and with a quarter of her coal left. It was then decided that it was better to build fairly large ships.

Steamships were soon coming into use

all over the world and were proving their worth. They made voyages possible at any time of the year. The trade winds no longer mattered. They were also very useful on inland water. This was very true in the USA whose long rivers were suitable for steamships. The old print (*left*) shows cotton being loaded onto such a ship on the Mississippi where most of the ships carried their paddle-wheels at the stern. All the early steamships were fitted with paddle-wheels, but this was not new. Drawings from the 6th century show similar side paddles being turned by men or animals. As early as 1817 there were at least five paddle boats driven by steam to be seen puffing along the Thames; there were even more in Scotland. In 1816 the **Elise** was the first steamship to cross the English Channel.

The first steam-propelled vessel in the Royal Navy was HMS **Diana** but it was soon realized that her paddles could easily be smashed by a well-aimed cannon-ball. However a Hendon scientist named F. P. Smith had invented the screw propeller. In 1837 this was tried on a launch and even when half of the propeller broke off the speed increased. So the navy decided to test it out. The paddle sloop **Alecto** had a tug-of-war with the screw-steamer **Rattler** (*above*). The **Rattler** won and soon all naval ships were propeller-driven.

A great inventor of the 19th century was Isambard Kingdom Brunel. He designed the **Great Western,** the first steamship to make regular voyages across the Atlantic. His next was the **Great Britain.** Built in 1845 she was the first all-iron, propeller-driven ship to cross the Atlantic. Although wrecked in the Falkland Islands in 1886 she was towed back to Bristol in 1970 and now lies in the same drydock in which she was built. In 1860 his wonder ship of the age made her appearance. She was the **Great Eastern** (*opposite*). She was a giant of a ship for her time – nearly six times larger than any other ship at that date. She was fitted with paddle-wheels, a propeller and sails. It would seem as if Brunel was ready to use almost every type of motive power, known to seamen. But, by the 1860s the propeller proved to be the most successful.

Many pleasure steamers carrying holidaymakers used paddle-wheels well into this century. (*Below*) the **Koh-i-Nor,** a typical British paddle-steamer of the early 1900s.

SHIPS IN BATTLE

When men first set out to sea they met and began to fight men of other tribes. In time these tribes became nations and the sea-fights grew larger. The first great naval battle in history was between the Greeks and the Persians at Salamis, in 480 BC and won by the new Athenian navy. The next great battle at sea was in 31 BC when the fleets of Antony and Cleopatra were defeated by a Roman fleet at Actium. One of the first battles fought in British home waters was in 885 AD when Alfred the Great smashed an invading Viking fleet off the Essex coast.

From then on, every century saw ships fighting ships. One great encounter was the battle of Lepanto in 1571. The Turks were proving a terror in the Mediterranean and had to be stopped. Don John of Austria led a

fleet of ships from many Christian nations and won a great victory. The number of Turkish dead was some 30,000 and dozens of their galleys were towed away as prizes. Although 286 Turkish ships fought in the battle, only 40 escaped. The battle, at its height, is seen (*below left*). (*Left*) a 24-pounder cannon brought up from the wreck of the Swedish warship **Vasa** which sank on her maiden voyage in 1628. It was guns, not unlike this cannon, which helped the British soundly defeat the 'invincible' Spanish Armada in 1588, a battle that is justly famous.

The following century saw a great number of naval battles between the British and the Dutch one of which, fought in June 1666, lasted for four days. When this war was over, the British next began to fight the French. For a while the fleets were led by one of the greatest naval commanders of all time – Horatio Nelson. He defeated the French at Aboukir Bay in 1798 and was at the bombardment of Trafalgar on October 21, 1805. His 27 ships, led into battle in two columns by his own **Victory,** defeated the combined French and Spanish fleets which numbered 33 ships, and saved England from possible invasion. He was killed by a marksman's bullet when victory was near. A fine painting of the Battle of Trafalgar is shown (*below*).

Ships of three nations joined forces – Britain, France and Russia – to fight a Turkish fleet at Navarino in 1827. It was a great victory for the allies and also was the last fleet action to be fought entirely by sailing ships.

For centuries, warships had always been wooden. Such ships were no longer built after 1859 when France's **La Gloire** and, in 1861, Britain's **Monarch** were the world's first ironclads, ships protected by iron plates. In 1862 the American Confederate ironclad **Merrimac** was defeated by a Northern ship, **Monitor,** fitted with a revolving turret.

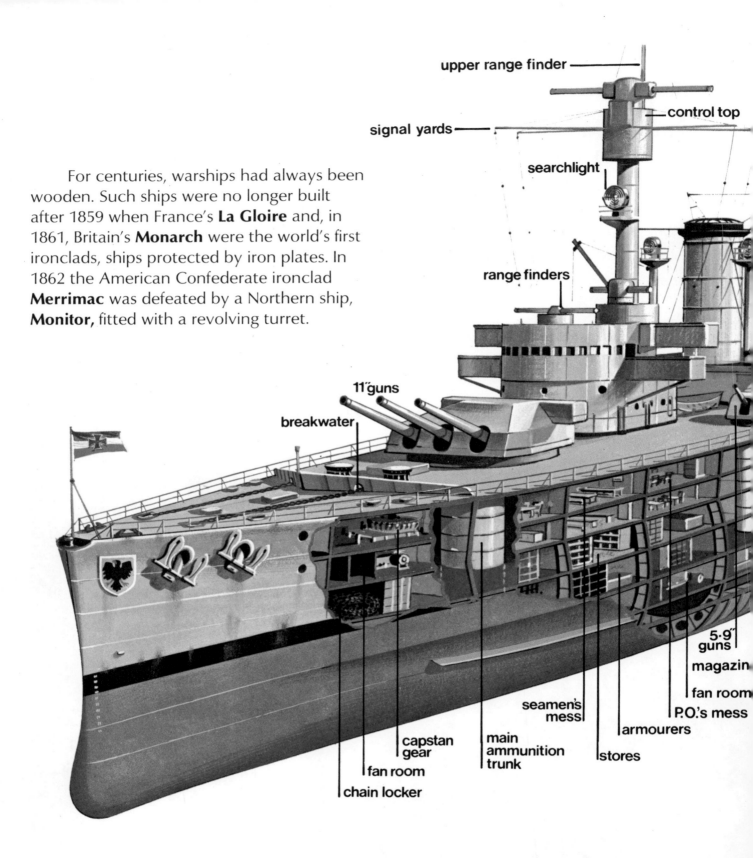

upper range finder

control top

signal yards

searchlight

range finders

11″guns

breakwater

5·9″ guns

magazin

fan room

P.O.'s mess

seamen's mess

armourers

capstan gear

main ammunition trunk

stores

fan room

chain locker

In 1870, HMS **Devastation** was the first British warship to be built without sails. From then on, warships of the world began to change completely, especially after the **Dreadnought** of 1906 and the coming of turbines. Warships also grew more complicated in design as can be seen in this cut-away section of the German battleship **Deutschland.** The first ship to carry an aircraft was the USS **Birmingham** in 1912. Soon a number of ships were being converted to aircraft carriers and today, such warships are usual. A typical carrier, the **HMS Ark Royal** is shown (*above right*).

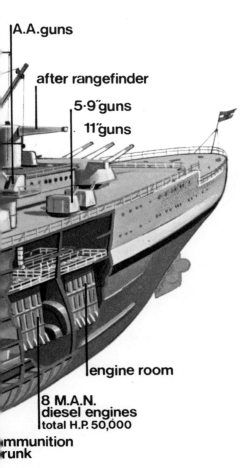

A.A.guns

after rangefinder

5·9″guns

11″guns

engine room

8 M.A.N.
diesel engines
total H.P. 50,000

mmunition
runk

Today's nuclear powered submarine
(*below*) has a striking power which is more
than all the explosives fired by all sides in the
two world wars.

THE LINERS

The success of the **Great Western** which crossed the Atlantic in 17 days much impressed a Canadian, Samuel Cunard. He sought and obtained a contract to carry mail across the North Atlantic and began to build four steam-driven ships. His first, the **Britannia,** made her maiden voyage on 4 July 1840, carrying passengers, cargo and mail. Despite a terrible storm she still managed to reach Halifax in 14 days 8 hours at an average speed of 8 knots. Soon all his four ships, now called Cunarders, were steaming between Liverpool and Boston (New York

came later) in all weathers. This was the first running-to-time passenger service across the Atlantic. His ships sailed every fortnight during eight months of the year and otherwise monthly. Although his ships were sometimes overtaken by fast clippers, his steamers could keep to a timetable for they did not depend on the wind.

In 1850, the American Collins Line challenged the Cunarders with the **Atlantic,** sailing from New York to Liverpool in under 11 days, at least half a day quicker than the fastest Cunarder. Cunard's reply was the **Persia,** his first iron ship, which crossed in

just over nine days. The race was on, a race which, in time, became known as the Blue Riband, an honour awarded to the ship making the fastest crossing. 1871 saw a new company, the White Star Line, with all its ships' names ending in 'ic'. One, the **Baltic,** cut the eastbound crossing to 7 days and 20 hours but the Cunard company came back with its first all-steel electricity-lit **Servia** which crossed in just under 7 days. Cunard also entered the **Mauretania** which held the Blue Riband from 1907 until 1929 – a wonderful record, especially as she bettered her times as she grew older.

Between the two world wars, the Atlantic trade boomed and European lines launched new and faster ships. Germany's **Bremen** broke the **Mauretania's** 22-year record, then Italy's **Rex,** France's **Normandie** and then Cunard's **Queen Mary** broke it in 1936. The last holder was the American liner, **United States.**

Today most passengers prefer to travel by jets which cross the Atlantic in hours. Much of the glamour and tradition of the giant liners has been lost. Today liners, such as the Italian **Raffaello,** (below), for the most part, are used for luxury cruising.

SPECIAL PURPOSE SHIPS AND BOATS

Few boats that were in use in the past exist today. An exception is the canoe – a craft that dates back as far as history. One of the earliest known is still used by the aborigines of Australia. It is made from a single sheet of eucalyptus bark, lashed together with strips of cane. Dug-out canoes are still used in the South Pacific with an outrigger to hold the

craft steady. The finest of all, however, are those of the American Indians, which are covered with birch bark or buffalo hides. A wooden paddle found in Yorkshire and dated 7,500 BC must have been used in a canoe. Canoes are also popular sport boats in many countries.

Another special purpose vessel is the lifeboat (above). Those of Britain were the world's first. The Royal Naval Lifeboat Institute (RNLI) was founded in 1824, and today they save well over a thousand people every year.

An early special purpose ship was designed to carry frozen meat. The first British ship to carry refrigerated meat from Britain to America was the **Circassia,** in 1879. The following year the **Strathleven** arrived in Britain with a cargo of Australian mutton. Then came the tank-steamers which carried bulk oil. Before then all liquid cargo had to be carried in barrels which were more work to load and unload. The growth of the oil industry resulted in tankers which also carried a variety of other liquid cargoes – wine and some acids for example.

To cut the costs of loading and unloading and to avoid theft, the modern container ship has come into use. The cargo is taken aboard in huge containers. Some are also roll-on/roll-off container ships which carry such cargoes as large lorries and heavy equipment and have huge cranes and fork lift trucks. One such ship, the **Atherstone,** is shown (below right). It can carry nearly 44,000 tonnes of cargo.

The real giants of the sea today are the oil tankers, yet the first was built in 1886. As the number of motor cars increased, so tankers were made larger to satisfy the growing need for more petrol. An average tanker of 1939 carried 13,000 tonnes of oil. By the 1960s this capacity had grown to over 100,000 tonnes and today some are reaching a fantastic half a million tonnes deadweight. The Shell tanker, **Marinula** (centre right).

Another special purpose ship is the ferry which, in the middle of the 19th

century began to carry wheeled vehicles across rivers. Today they are capable of carrying huge lorries. Another type of ferry is the air cushion vehicle, better known as the hovercraft. The first was built in Britain in 1959. The hovercraft is neither ship nor aircraft but something in between, riding over water on a cushion of air *(above)*.

Equally important will be underwater ships to recover the treasure that lies on the world's ocean beds. The South Pacific alone, it is estimated, contains nearly two million tonnes of material which contains many valuable metals, such as manganese, copper, nickel and so on. Each kind of raw material may be worth a great deal. Now all that remains is for some scientist to invent a kind of vacuum cleaner that will 'sweep' the ocean beds clean of the riches that wait below.

MARINULA
LONDON

BOATS FOR PLEASURE

Yachting has been enjoyed in Britain for at least three centuries. Early in his reign, King Charles II introduced the first yacht from Holland. That was in 1661. The world's first yacht club was the Water-Club of Cork, which began in 1720. Yet the Royal Thames Yacht Club may claim the longest ancestry in Great Britain. It was founded in 1777 when the Duke of Cumberland offered a cup to be raced for on the Thames. Today, yachting has grown into one of the most popular sports in many countries.

Once every two years during August

yachts from all over the world meet at Cowes, Isle of Wight, for one of the premier ocean racing events – the Admiral's Cup. Another great yacht race is the America's Cup. It first began in 1851 and the trophy has been held by the USA ever since. The Observer newspaper now sponsors a single-handed race across the Atlantic every four years. But yachting is now a sport for all who enjoy being on the water.

On the right track

GETTING UP STEAM

The great English inventor, James Watt, made railways possible. He was the first to harness steam and in 1774 made a steam pumping engine, the principles of which are still used today. Richard Trevithick of Cornwall used steam and in 1804 built his first 'railway' engine. But it had little power and could not be used for hauling.

The most famous railway pioneer was George Stephenson. Having invented a number of engines his opportunity came when it was decided to build a 42km (26 mile) railway from Stockton to Darlington to carry coal. This stretch of railway was opened on 27 September 1825 (*opposite*). It was a great success. On that day the railway age truly began. A typical engine of those early days (*above*). Early prints (*below*) show how passengers and goods were carried.

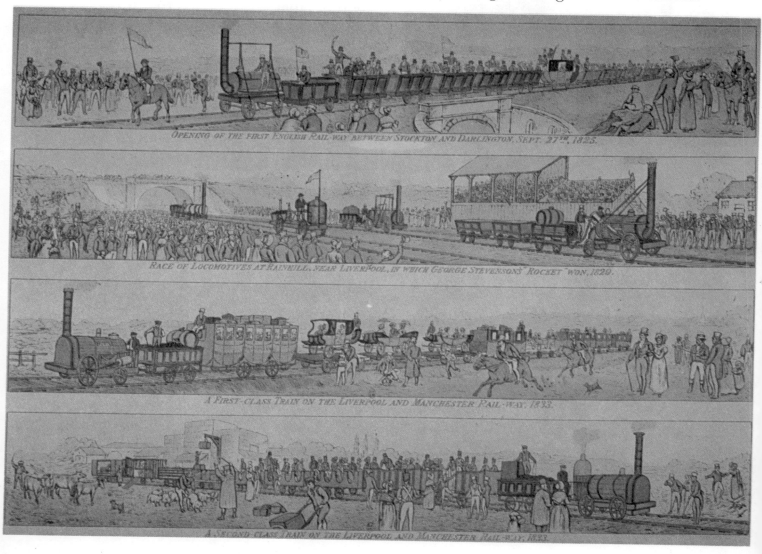

OPENING OF THE FIRST ENGLISH RAIL-WAY BETWEEN STOCKTON AND DARLINGTON, SEPT. 27TH, 1825.

RACE OF LOCOMOTIVES AT RAINHILL, NEAR LIVERPOOL, IN WHICH GEORGE STEVENSON'S ROCKET WON, 1829.

A FIRST-CLASS TRAIN ON THE LIVERPOOL AND MANCHESTER RAIL-WAY, 1833.

A SECOND-CLASS TRAIN ON THE LIVERPOOL AND MANCHESTER RAIL-WAY, 1833.

THE GOLDEN AGE OF RAIL

The next important railway line to be built in England was that between the manufacturing centre of Manchester and the seaport of Liverpool. With such a railway, raw cotton could be brought to Manchester, turned into bales of cloth, and then these could be carried back to Liverpool for export. Once again George Stephenson was placed in charge. His men laid more than 48km (30 miles) of double track – the most ambitious railway scheme at that time. The worst obstacle was Chat Moss, a huge area of swampland. But Stephenson was not put out by this challenge although when he first stepped onto it he sank up to his knees. 'We shall meet Moss with moss', he said and a 'road' of dried moss, wooden hurdles and tree branches was laid. For this new track he designed the world's most famous locomotive – the **Rocket** – which can be seen in London's Science Museum.

The line was opened on 25 September 1830, to scenes of great excitement, marred by an unfortunate accident that caused the death of William Huskisson, MP for Liverpool who stepped in the path of an oncoming train. For this otherwise grand opening George Stephenson gained his title – 'Father of the Railway'. Slowly but surely a network of railway lines began to spread across Britain. Although the trains were meant for the carriage of goods, it was not long before passengers were eager to be carried by the snorting, puffing little engines. The carriages, however, were at first far from comfortable. There were three classes, and the third class carriages were no better than trucks, with no seats and open to the sky. Yet these trains became more and more popular. Some were highly decorated as the picture (*left*) shows, and much more comfortable (*bottom*). By then, in 1842, the railway had carried its most famous passenger of that time, Queen Victoria. After that railways became even more popular. After all, they were able to cover distances in better time and more comfort than had been known before.

The railway on which Queen Victoria had travelled was the work of Britain's greatest 19th century engineer – Isambard Kingdom Brunel – who was in charge of the line that ran to the west country. The trains on this were often halted by earth slipping from the cliffs beside the track. Such a landslide, near Dawlish, is shown (*opposite above*).

And so the golden years continued. In 1975 there was a great 150th anniversary pageant and, (*below right*) is shown a 'Jubilee' class **Leander** on its way to Darlington to join in the pageant celebrating those early days.

DRAWING ROOM CAR-FOLKESTONE EXPRESS
SOUTH EASTERN & CHATHAM RAILWAY

LARGE AND SMALL

By the time Queen Victoria had taken her first train journey, the railway network was beginning to spread across Britain. For years the countryside was filled with armies of 'navvies' digging cuttings, embankments and tunnels. It is said that in 1849 nearly 200,000 men were at work. In 1844 a law known as Gladstone's Cheap Trains Act meant that the railway companies had to run a certain number of trains daily. Third class passengers went for a penny a mile and also had to be carried in covered trucks. Of course, these early travellers did not have corridor trains, sleeping or dining cars or toilets. Fortunately most trains stopped at every station allowing passengers to get off, buy something to eat and see to their other needs.

Heating, too, was another problem. In cold weather the poor passengers wrapped themselves up and put their feet into muffs. Eventually ways were found to use the heat

of the engines to heat carriages.

The number of people using the trains increased – and so did the size of the engines – despite several serious accidents. The worst was in December 1879 when a gale blew down the Tay Bridge in Scotland, together with the train passing over it at the time.

Not discouraged by this disaster, the various railway companies built larger and more powerful engines to try to beat each other's times. A typical giant, **King George V** is shown (*opposite*), yet small and delightful little engines were being built also. (*Opposite below*) the Bluebell Railway, built in 1901 and still used to carry holidaymakers. Another is the famous Welsh Talyllyn Railway. On this page are shown two overseas 'giants'. (*Right*) **The Canadian** passing through the Rockies, and (*below*) a **Union Pacific** 8,500 horse-power locomotive heading for Wyoming.

AROUND THE WORLD

It was not long before the rest of the world saw the advantages of railways, especially in the USA where the huge distances across the continent seemed shortened by the railway. North America's transcontinental railway system was begun in 1864 to cross the country from the Pacific to the Atlantic. The workers moving inland from the east were mainly Irishmen; those from the west coast were Chinese. Some 10,000 men were put to work. The weather was oven-hot in the deserts and freezing cold when crossing the Sierra Mountains. Some men froze where they stood; often the men had to drop their tools and pick up rifles to fight off bands of Indians. But the two sets of rails met at last. The next day the last spike was driven in – a spike of gold – and the two engines that had travelled with the crew faced each other, their giant 'cowcatchers' touching. By 1872 the American railway network totalled 112,000km (70,000 miles).

(Above) one of the three 2-6-2 narrow

gauge locos operated by British Rail in Wales and (below) locomotive No. 107 about 12,000km (7,500 miles) away, on the Huantayo-Huantavelica Railway, Peru.

Railways were soon being built by other great nations, especially in Australasia, South

America and the Far East. In Australia, for example, a continent of nearly 7,770,000 square kilometres (3,000,000 square miles), only railways could link the various cities, many of which are hundreds of kilometres apart. New Zealand soon began to develop its own railway system, and we show (right) modernized rolling stock, pulled by an American type Da class locomotive. In Japan, there were once many fine steam engines but these are now being scrapped. A recent victim was the C62 passenger engine (above). India had the problem of her high mountains. An Indian train (below) is battling its way upwards through the many curves of the Darjeeling-Himalaya Railway.

THE UNUSUAL

Trains were first used only to carry goods from one point to another, usually on level ground. Then special compartments were built to carry passengers. As railways increased, so did their designs, for it was soon seen how many different jobs they could do. For example, a 70-year-old engine is seen hauling molten slag from a German steelworks (*above*).

Mountain railways have proved very popular, especially at places such as ski-resorts like those of Switzerland. They save the skiers from having to trudge to the top of the mountain before ski-ing down again. Such mountain railways are worked by cable. In earlier railways the cars were fixed to cables which hauled them up and down by winding gear which was at both the top and bottom of the track. Today, however, the cables are fixed and each car has its own electrically operated trolley. The first mountain railway in Europe was the Vitnau-Rigi in Switzerland. This was opened in 1871 and electrified in 1937.

One strange looking railway is the monorail. This has carriages suspended under the rail and is able to carry its passengers between short stops at great speeds. There have been many types of monorail including one, tried out in Scotland in 1930, which was driven by propellors like an aeroplane. A very famous monorail railway is that over the River Wupper in Germany. It was built in 1903 and has been running ever since. Another type of railway is the rack railway; one of the ten such motor coaches used on the Pilatus rack railway in Switzerland is shown (*left*).

1883 and is still very popular. However, special purpose trains are usually designed for work. One (*above right*) is carrying sugar cane on a narrow gauge railway in Queensland, Australia. Other trains in Queensland have been designed to haul cattle, moving about 3,000,000 head yearly. Wagons also are designed for special purposes – petrol carriers, refrigerated containers and so on. There is hardly any limit to the variety of these 'specials'. One is shown (*below*), a snow plough at Klosters in Switzerland.

In addition to the railways built for tourists in the mountains, there are others to give pleasure to people at the seaside. At one time almost all the large seaside resorts around Britain had coastal railways. A recent picture (*above left*), shows Volk's electric railway which was opened in Brighton in

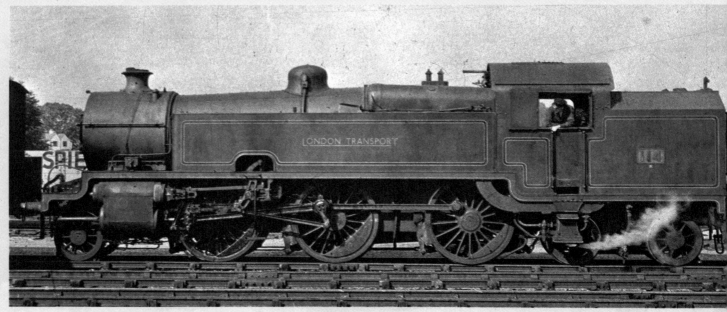

TRAINS GO UNDERGROUND

At the beginning of the 19th century, traffic was a great problem in many cities throughout the world. This was especially true in London. In 1843, Charles Pearson, a London lawyer had the idea that a railway should be built under the streets, to relieve the traffic jams. A great deal of talk followed and finally digging began in 1860. The method used was known as 'cut and cover'. A deep, open trench was dug, roofed over with brick, then covered with earth. In the tunnel that was formed, tracks were laid and steam locomotives ran along them. The first part of the track was laid from Paddington to the City of London. It was called the Metropolitan Line and is now the northern half of the Circle Line. Despite clouds of choking smoke, it was a great success. About 30,000 people were carried over that line during the very first day. In fact, from 9 o'clock in the morning until past noon it was difficult to find a place in any of the carriages going to the City. In the evening the rush reversed and the crowd at the City end was almost impossible to control. That first day proved to everyone that there was a great future for 'Underground' trains. Soon lines were sprouting in all directions. Opposite are shown Blackfriars Station in 1875 (*above*) and an early train (*below*). After a while the 'cut and cover' system was found to take too

long and a new style of tunnels, bored at a deeper level, came into being. These were part of the underground system and gained the name of the 'Tube'. The first ran from King William Street in the City, beneath the River Thames, to Stockwell, about 5.2km ($3\frac{1}{4}$ miles). This was the world's first railway to use electricity. The Central Lines of 9.5km (6 miles) which followed, became known as the 'Twopenny Tube' because at first a standard fare of 2 pennies (less than 1p) was charged for any distance travelled along the route.

Since those early days London's Underground system has spread until it reaches far out into the suburbs. The most used station is Victoria which has some 46,000,000 passengers every year out of a total of some 546,000,000. As in the case of the railways, London's Underground system soon began to be copied by other nations. The first underground railway on the continent of Europe was in Budapest in 1896. The **Metro** of Paris began in 1898, Berlin had its **U-bahn** in 1902 and in 1898 America's first Subway opened in Boston. New York had its first Subway system six years later, because something of the city's traffic problem had been eased by its elevated railroads. Today, however, it is the largest in the world. Other cities in North America – Centre Station, Washington DC is shown – (*left*) South America and Japan have underground railways, and that in Moscow, built in the 1930s, has what are regarded as the world's most beautiful stations.

MODERN RAILWAYS AND THE FUTURE

The highest speed recorded by a steam locomotive was 201·6 km/hr (126 mph), by the **Mallard** in 1938. But speed was sacrificed, slowly giving way to diesels which were more economical. Since then gas turbines have come into use. The American Union Pacific Railroad has several mammoth engines powered by this method. Most of Britain's main lines are now completely electrified, her locomotives mostly diesel-electrics.

There is every possibility, however, that trains of the future will be based on the hovercraft invented in 1953. They will have no wheels or the usual type of track and will reach speeds of up to 480 km/hr (300 mph). As there is no contact between the train and the track such high speeds are quite possible. Already tests are going on in Britain and the USA and the result may well affect all trains we shall see in the future.

Three British express trains (*opposite*). (*Left*) a diesel-electric locomotive and (*right*) a typical modern passenger train at speed. (*Below*) a British high-speed train which can often reach 200 km/hr (125 mph). (*Above*) a modern dome car and, (*below*), the new 'cowl type' American diesel locomotives.

The horseless carriage

THE STEAMERS

If George Stephenson may be called the 'Father of the Railways', so a Frenchman, Nicholas Cugnot may be called 'The First Motorist'. He tested out his first carriage, in 1793. The machine ran well but crashed into a wall. Another attempt ended when the machine overturned. Poor Cugnot was put into prison. The next horseless carriage that worked was designed by Richard Trevithick, of railway fame. A few days later he and a few friends went to celebrate his success in an inn. But the boiler of the steam-car ran dry, blew up, and Britain's first self-propelled carriage was scattered in all directions.

More and more men saw the value of steam carriages. Sir Goldsworthy Gurney and Walter Hancock were two, and a third, Dr Church, ran a regular steam-carriage service from London to Birmingham. Yet the days of the steam driven carriages were ending although, in the USA, they lingered on with the Stanley Steamers, speedy, powerful and silent. A typical 'steamer' is the **de Dion-Bouton,** (below). A Peugeot of 1891 (right).

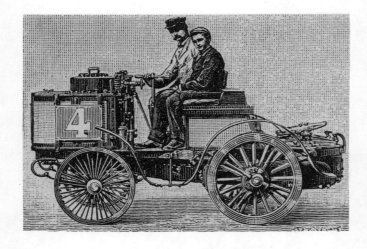

PETROL TAKES OVER

Until 1865, English vehicles led the world. Then, because of the Red Flag Act which limited vehicles to 6·5 km/hr (4 mph), Continental designers took the lead. Steam was still used until, in Germany in 1886, Gottlieb Daimler fitted a carriage with a petrol engine. It made history, being the true ancestor of the modern car. The first man to make petrol cars for sale was another German, Karl Benz, who was experimenting at the same time as Daimler and, in 13 years, sold more than 2,300 very simple but reliable cars. But French and Italian companies also entered this new and exciting field. A **Daimler** car of 1899 is shown (below). Opposite, a **Fiat** of 1901 (above) and a racing model, the **Fiat S74** (below).

CARS FOR THE FAMILY

For a long time motoring was a rich man's luxury, for the high cost of cars meant that few could afford them. Then, in 1904, an attempt was made to produce a car that was low priced. It was the **Brushmobile,** a 6 horse-power car with a Vauxhall engine. It was not very successful, but a start had been made. As more cars were being built and sold prices tumbled and by 1914 a light car could be run quite cheaply. Cars had finally lost that 'horseless carriage' look. At the same time automobile engines were improving. In the USA in 1914 Henry Ford began to mass produce cheap cars for millions of Americans; in Britain, William Morris did the same for the British. In 1913 he brought out his first 'bull-nose' **Morris Oxford** which soon became as familiar in Britain as Ford's **Model T** in the USA. With it, motoring came to the average man and his family. Half a million Model T's were sold in 1916. By 1927 when its production stopped, Ford had sold 15 million. Another famous British name at this time was the **Vauxhall,** which first appeared in 1903.

In Europe, the French **Bugatti,** Italian **Alfa Romeo** and the German **Mercedes** were also becoming very popular. An **Alfa Romeo** of 1910 is shown (below). (Opposite), the popular, low-priced **Austin 7,** known affectionately as the 'baby' Austin and (below) a 1927 **Vauxhall.**

MOTORING FOR THE MILLIONS

When designing his **Model T,** Henry Ford told the world what he intended to do. 'I will build a motor car for the great multitude,' he said. 'It will be large enough for the family, but small enough for the individual to run and care for it. It will be so low in price that no man making a good salary will be unable to own one – and enjoy with his family the blessings of hours of pleasure in God's open places.' Prophetic words indeed. He, together with the great European car-makers, was to make those words come true. This was especially so during the years 1919 to 1930, for these were the years when both cars and roads improved greatly. But soon the gentle, ambling family car was joined by the first of the sports cars. From the works of William Morris (later Lord Nuffield) came a number of MG sports cars which included the famous **Midget** of 1929. Other fine British sports cars, but of a different price range, were the 4½ litre **Bentley,** first seen in 1919, and also the **Alvis, Aston Martin** and **Lagonda.**

It became very obvious that roads generally could not cope with this increasing traffic and the now familiar 'trunk' roads had to be built. The family cars remained the most popular. This was particularly true after 1945 when Britain had to face competition from abroad. One foreign car (*opposite below*) was the **Volkswagen 'Beetle',** from Germany, but 'experts' declared it was 'of no technical or practical merit.' It had been designed by Ferdinand Porsche, a man responsible for many successful cars. This car, 'of no technical merit' has sold over 19 million all over the world, in the 25 years since it was introduced. Ford cars too became very popular; a huge factory to make them in Britain was erected in Essex. (*Opposite top left*), a 1953 **Anglia** and **Prefect** model, both of which were sold in thousands. In the 1960s, cars began to arrive from Japan. (*Opposite top right*) the 180B **Datsun Bluebird** which has a top speed of 166 km/hr (103 mph).

CARS OF TODAY – AND TOMORROW

It is incredible to think that the motor car is only about a hundred years old. At first, as we have seen, it was a luxury. In the USA, for example, 600 were made in 1899. Twenty-five years later the number was little short of 20 million. Today, on the motorways of the world, 100 million cars are in daily use. It has been said that in Britain and America there are enough cars to carry the whole population of both countries.

Methods of manufacture have changed little over the past few years but it seems possible that future cars may be powered by gas-turbines. The world's first turbine car was built by Britain's Rover company and then succeeded by the **Rover/BRM.** Other car manufacturers have been looking back to the days of the electric cars, but with a difference, for it is hoped that a small, powerful and long-lasting battery, that may be plugged in to recharge overnight will be invented. This will result in power for local journeys and a great saving in petrol. But that is in the future. The **Ford Fiesta** (below) gives the possible shape of a car in the years ahead. (Below) is the **Cadillac Eldorado,** the largest-engined production car in the world.

CAR AGAINST CAR

The first motor trial was in France, a race between two automobiles, known as the Paris/Rouen trials. The prize was shared between Panhard and Levassor in one car and the Peugeot brothers in the other. Watching the race was an American newspaper owner, James Gordon Bennett.

He became so excited that the following year he organized a more ambitious event, for the Gordon Bennett Cup. Twenty-two cars took part and drove from Paris to Bordeaux and back. Nine finished and the winner was Emile Levassor in his Daimler-engined **Panhard.** In 1900, a car salesman named Emil Jellinek built racing cars lower

and with a longer wheel base, naming them **Mercedes** after his young daughter. From those early days Grand Prix racing developed. The first race in 1906, was won by a **Renault** at an average speed of 100·8 km/hr (63 mph) over 1,232 km (770 miles) of terrible roads. After that, special racing tracks were built. Brooklands, in Britain, was opened a year later in 1907.

The 1977 Grand Prix champion is Niki Lauda. His rivals include Mario Andretti, Jody Scheckter and James Hunt.

(*Opposite above*) a **D-type Jaguar,** (*opposite below*) an **Alpine A220.** Former world champion Emerson Fittipaldi (*above*) and the S bends in the 70s (*below*).

THE SPEEDSTERS

It was only natural that the early sportsman, having a car, wanted to see how fast it would go. Soon a rivalry sprang up all over the world to decide who owned the fastest. Such efforts were not against other cars – but against the clock! The first such recorded time was in 1898 when a Frenchman, Chasseloup-Laubat, driving a **Jeantaud,** reached the dizzy speed of 62·9 km/hr (39·3 mph). He, and another Frenchman, Jenatzy, driving a car of his own design, broke the record five times in turn during 1899. Indeed, it was to be Frenchmen who held the world's speed record until 1903 when a man with a familiar name, Henry Ford, broke it with a speed of 146·1 km/hr (91·3 mph). At this time a young man named C. S. Rolls had tried to beat the record with three attempts. He finally gave up and went into partnership with another to produce cars – the **Rolls-Royce.** The attempts went on. In 1904 history was made when Louis Rigolly broke the 'ton' barrier with a speed of 165·6 km/hr (103·5 mph).

World War I put a stop to record-breaking for a while. The next, in 1922, was made by K. L. Guinness in a **Sunbeam** at 213·9 km/hr (133.7 mph). Now it became Britain's turn. Men like Malcolm Campbell, Henry Segrave, Parry-Thomas, George Eyston and John Cobb continually broke the record during the 1920s, 1930s and 1940s; Cobb reaching 630 km/hr (393·8 mph) on the Bonneville Salt Flats, in the USA in 1947. In 1964 Donald Campbell (son of Malcolm) became the first person to exceed 640 km/hr (400 mph) doing 403·1 mph in his **Bluebird II** at Lake Eyre, Australia. Since then, American drivers have held the speed record. Craig Breedlove was the first to break 800 km/hr (500 mph) in 1964 and then 960 km/hr (600 mph) in the following year. The current world record is held by Gary Gabelich who recorded 1,008·6 km/hr (630·38 mph) at Bonneville in 1970. He and his amazing car, **Blue Flame,** are shown (*opposite*).

MOTORCYCLES

In addition to being among the first men to produce a successful motor car, Gottlieb Daimler was one of the very first to make the earliest motor cycle. His 'wooden wonder', produced in 1885, is shown, (*right*). Slowly the motorcycles became better designed and faster-engined. A later machine is the **Nimbus** (*far right*) with a shaft drive and telescopic front fork. Today motorcycles are reliable, fast and often luxurious. One outstanding machine is the 1,000 cc **BMW** (*below*) which has a twin-cylinder engine and shaft-drive to the rear wheel.

    Toughness of modern machines is proved by trials riding. A Montesas is shown over a typically rough course (*below right*).

Into the sky

The idea of flying has fascinated people from the beginning of time. The first successful flights were made in a hot-air balloon, a model of which was demonstrated in 1709 by Bartolomeu de Gusmao. No one seemed interested and it was not until November 1783 that man actually rose from the ground. This was in a hot-air balloon made by the Montgolfier brothers. Their balloon (*left*) carrying Pilátre de Rozier and the Marquis d'Arlandes, flew over Paris. A few days later Jacques Charles made the first voyage in a hydrogen balloon. Flying had begun!

By the 19th century, parachuting was added to air shows when ascents in balloons had lost their excitement. The first parachute was designed by Leonardo da Vinci in the 15th century. A 'Red Devil' and his parachute (*below*). A modern hot air balloon (*right*).

The balloon raised man from the ground, but he had not flown, merely floated. Henri Giffard changed that. In 1852 he designed a balloon that was shaped rather like a rugby football, fixed a 3 hp steam engine beneath, and flew from Paris to Trappes at 9·5 km/hr (6 mph). The greatest of the early airship men, however, was a Brazilian Alberto Santos-Dumont. He invented a number of power-driven airships and in one, **No. 6,** of 1901 he flew round the Eiffel Tower *(left)*. Another great name was that of Count Zeppelin who built huge airships that bore his name. One of his largest, **Hindenburg,** was destroyed by fire at Lakehurst, New Jersey *(above)*. Hang-gliding, a popular modern sport *(below)* was first tried in the late 19th century.

THE FIRST FLIGHTS

The next stage in the history of flight was for man to fly in a heavier-than-air machine. The great pioneer in this field was a German, Otto Lilienthal who, in 1896, was on the point of making the world's first such powered flight when he was killed. On his grave was written the phrase – 'Sacrifices must be made' – his own words. News of his work reached two young brothers, Orville and Wilbur Wright in the USA. They had been experimenting with a flying machine and Lilienthal's work inspired them to carry on from where he had so sadly left off. By 1903 they had made a flying machine of wood, string and canvas with a 12 hp motor and two chain driven propellers. They called it the **Flyer.** They took it to Kitty Hawk, North Carolina where they flipped a coin. Orville, having won the toss, climbed onto the pilot's wooden seat. The machine rested on a trolley set on a crude railway track and a cord from this trolley led to a weight hanging from a tower nearby. This was to assist in take-off. Wilbur swung the propellers, the engine spluttered into life and when the weight crashed down, the machine sped along the rails and, at the end, became smoothly airborne. It was in the air for 12 seconds – but those were 12 of the most important seconds in history. It was then Wilbur's turn (*above*), the brothers making two flights each. The longest was 59 seconds at 48 km/hr (30 mph). On that day, 17 December 1903, the air had been conquered at last.

News of the success reached Europe and encouraged others. The first was Santos-Dumont, the airship designer. He stayed airborne in his machine, a kind of box-kite with a motor, for 21 seconds. The following year Henry Farman made the first circular flight of more than a kilometre in Europe.

Britain's first official flight was made by an American, S. F. Cody, in 1908. In 1909 an Anglo-Frenchman, Hubert Latham, tried to fly the English Channel, but came down in

the sea. He was rescued safely. Louis Blériot, a Frenchman, became the first man to fly across the Channel, a trip that took him 37 minutes on 25 July 1909. Suddenly, it seemed, Britain was no longer an island! The first international air show was held at Rheims, France in August, 1909. Farman won the endurance prize for a 180km (112mile) flight and Glenn Curtiss won the speed prize at 70km/hr (43mph).

Soon the flying craze was sweeping the world. In the USA in 1911, Galbraith Rodgers flew right across the country, completing the journey in 49 days. In that year also the first air mail service began. Nations also began to realize what use the aeroplane could be in time of war and Britain's Royal Flying Corps was formed in 1912. Other countries soon did the same. But aircraft, like balloons, were at first merely to spy on the enemy. The dream that the Wright brothers had brought to reality – 'heavier-than-air' powered flying – had started something. Many types of aircraft began to be built. (*Opposite*) an early **Avro** triplane.

WORLD WAR I

World War I began in 1914 and ended in 1918. Invention and design are often prodded on by war and this war was no exception. When it began, aircraft were flimsy machines of wood and canvas. Within four short years they were changed into fast, modern-looking fighting planes and into the bombers which were to become the airliners in time of peace. Before 1914 aircraft had been built in very small numbers, often by a few men in tiny workshops. Suddenly, the whole picture changed, and they began to pour out of factories in vast numbers that steadily increased.

From being an untried machine, good only for spying out the enemy's movements, the aeroplane grew into a fighting machine to be reckoned with, one that could even turn the tide of battles. Yet when the war began, not a single aeroplane had been designed for aerial combat. Instead, at first, they were slow, unarmed scouts. Usually, when an Allied pilot met a German pilot he would wave to him with a friendly greeting. Then machine guns were added and 'dogfights' in the sky became common. Bombers, too, began to be built, striking at places many kilometres behind the trenches that marked the front line. Later in the war they were also used to torpedo ships and to sink submarines.

Airships, too, were used, mainly for coastal patrol or for escorting convoys. In Britain they first came under the command of the Royal Naval Air Service which joined the Royal Flying Corps in 1918 to become the Royal Air Force. By then there had been many 'knights of the air'. Among the most famous were Manfred von Richthofen of Germany (80 victories) who flew a triplane like the one (*below left*), and Edward

Mannock of Britain (73 victories) who flew the **Sopwith Camel,** one of the finest planes of the war (*below right*). It shot down more enemy aircraft than any other fighter. Canada's ace was Billy Bishop (72 victories) who actually survived the war. Edward Rickenbacker, the ace of the USA (26 victories) flew a **Nieuport** 28 and his greatest month was October 1918 when he shot down 14 enemy aircraft. One of the French aces was Georges Huynemer. During the course of 600 flights he shot down 54 enemy planes. In 1915 a Dutchman, Anthony Fokker, produced a monoplane which destroyed many Allied machines until answered by the **British Pups, Camels** and **SE5As** and French **Spads** and **Nieuports.**

(*Overleaf*) a squadron of **DH4** light bombers closing up to fight off an attack by biplanes and **Fokker** triplanes.

WORLD SHRINKERS

When World War I ended on 11 November 1918, flying was once again a peacetime job. There were hundreds of experienced pilots and thousands of bombers which could easily be turned into carriers of people and goods. While government leaders were discussing how best to use this material, there came something which staggered the world. Two Englishmen, John Alcock and Arthur Whitten-Brown made the first non-stop flight across the Atlantic in a war-time **Vickers Vimy** bomber in less than 17 hours. This made everyone realize that, thanks to the aeroplane, the world had suddenly become a much smaller place. Having seen what could be done, many other bombers were altered to do civilian work. One was the French **Farman Goliath** which began a regular air service between London and Paris. Another was the **Handley Page** which,

in time, became the main aircraft in the Imperial Airways fleet, the forerunner of British Airways. Another valuable plane was the American **Ford Trimotor** nicknamed 'Tin Goose' (below).

There were many trail-blazers in these inter-war years. Charles Lindbergh made the first solo crossing of the Atlantic in May 1927. Charles Kingsford-Smith and Charles Ulm flew the Pacific, and in 1933 the American pilot, Wiley Post, was the first to fly solo round the world. In 1930 Amy Johnson flew solo from England to Australia in 20 days and Amelia Earhart flew non-stop across the Atlantic in 1928 and disappeared while flying around the world in 1937.

Flying-boats (opposite above) and **Zeppelins** were being used for the Atlantic crossing as was the new **Boeing 247** (opposite below) the father of modern transport aircraft.

WORLD WAR II

Hardly had the air routes become established when in September 1939 the world again plunged into war. This time the warring nations were prepared with vicious fighters and huge bombers able to carry tonnes of deadly bombs. It was a frightening prospect. With the help of her bombers, Germany overran Poland and then invaded Belgium, Holland, France and northern Europe. Soon only the British Royal Air Force remained to face the attacks of Germany's Luftwaffe. But in 1940 the Battle of Britain was won and then, from May 1942 onwards, British and American bombers droned over Germany, dropping well over a million tonnes of bombs. Meanwhile, war had begun

in the Pacific when Japanese aircraft attacked Pearl Harbor.

Three of the Second World War's outstanding aircraft. (*Above*) a **Spitfire** banks sharply. (*Opposite right*) two **Hurricanes** fly together in close formation. (*Below*) the **American DC-3 (Dakota),** the most famous transport plane of the war.

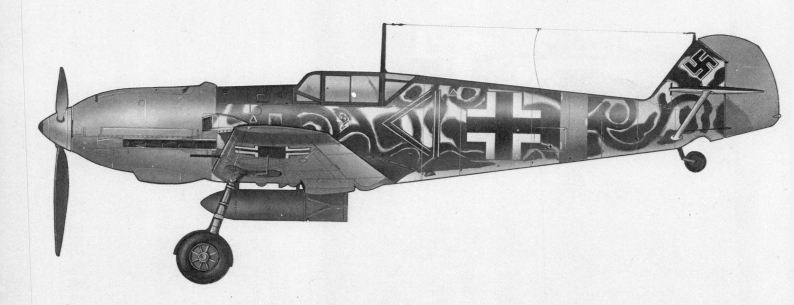

World War II ended in 1945 when atom bombs were dropped on Hiroshima and Nagasaki, Japan. It had been very much an aerial war, with some 750,000 aircraft taking part. What were the outstanding planes included among them? Already mentioned (*previous page*) were the **Spitfire, Hurricane** and **Dakota.** The **Messerschmitt Me 109** (*above*) was the one most widely used by the Luftwaffe, serving on nearly every front, although the **Focke-Wulf** was a better machine.

Another great fighter-plane was Japan's **Mitsubishi Zero-Sen** (*above right*). America's

Mustang, and Russia's **Mikoyan/Gurevich,** the famous **MiG,** a successful fighter-bomber.

The war's outstanding bombers were Britain's **Lancaster,** the aircraft that took part in the 'Dam-Busters' raid and the attack on the **Tirpitz,** and the **de Havilland Mosquito,** ideal for fast, low-level attacks. There were also the **Heinkel,** Germany's finest medium bomber and the American **Boeing B17,** or 'Flying Fortress' (below). And the men who flew them? The greatest ace of the war was Germany's Walter Nowotny who shot down an amazing total of 258 planes. Britain's leading ace was 'Johnnie' Johnson who chalked up 38 victories. He flew on 515 missions, and his plane was only hit once. Another great British pilot was Douglas Bader who, despite the loss of both legs, still flew bombers. The Frenchman, Pierre Clostermann flew with the RAF and scored 33 victories. Richard Bong, America's most successful ace shot down 40 enemy planes. Ivan Koxhedub, Russia's top ace, shot down 62. There were many other devoted pilots.

THE JET AGE ARRIVES

Jet-engined aircraft did not play a very important part in World War II. The first to appear were the **Messerschmitt Me 163,** called the **Komet,** and the **Me 262** twin-jet fighter bomber. About 370 **Komets** were built but did not prove very successful – they were too fast to hit slow-flying bombers! The Allies' answer was the **Gloster E28/39** (*below*) powered by a Whittle jet. However it arrived too late to have much effect on aerial warfare.

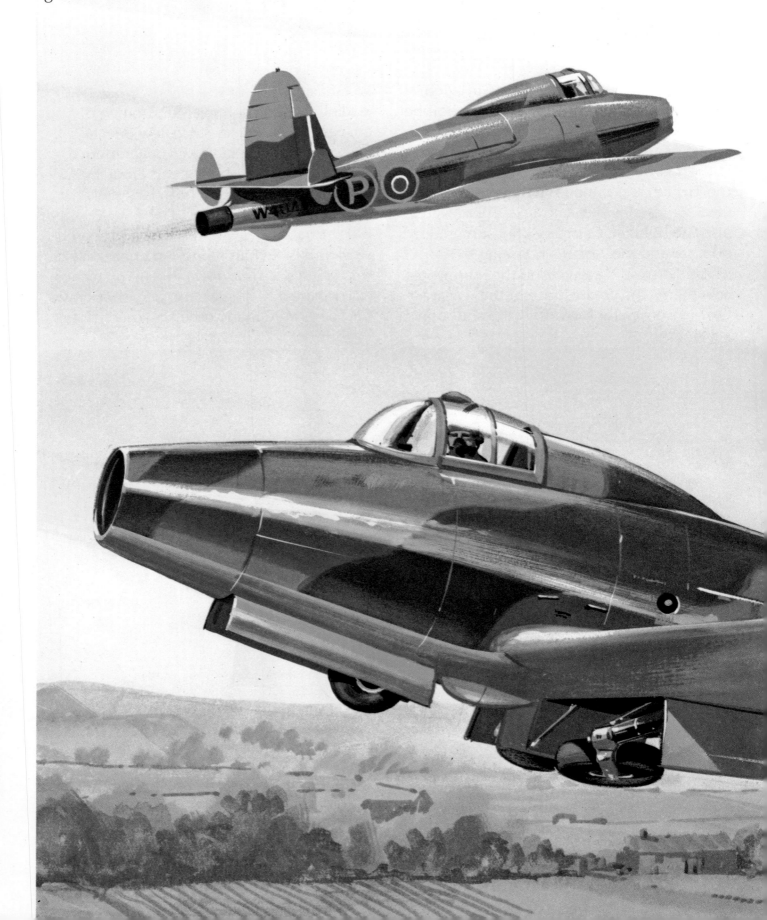

As people were to realize, World War II had done much for aviation. Flying was, without doubt, a safe and reliable means of travelling from one place to another. Governments had done a great deal to bring this about, in the designing and testing of aircraft, and in building airports throughout the world. True, they had been built for military aircraft – fighters and bombers – but it was not a difficult matter to change them so that they could handle civilian planes. The same was true of the many factories that were scattered about Britain and the USA, especially of those belonging to the de Havilland Company. Four of them began work on a new and exciting airliner. The result was **Comet 1,** (*right*) which was to become the world's first jet-airliner. It was used on the service between Great Britain and Johannesburg which opened on 2 May 1952.

WATERBORNE AIRCRAFT

The idea of building aircraft that would land on water is very practical. After all, the sea apart, there are many lakes and inland waterways that make perfect, natural landing strips. In 1911 the US Navy ordered two seaplanes from Glenn Curtiss who had developed them for water take-offs.

Several types, in fact, were used during World War I. In May 1919, three big American tri-motor flying-boats set off to fly across the Atlantic, in stages. Two had to give up but the third, a **Navy Curtiss,** finally reached Plymouth to a great welcome. The following month, of course, Alcock and Brown flew the Atlantic non-stop to make aviation history. In 1924 two **Douglas World Cruisers** of the US Army made the first round-the-world flight. These were not exactly flying-boats, as such, but had two floats beneath the body of each plane so that they could easily land on the water's surface. Such a type is the **Gipsy Moth** (*below*). A similar sort of aircraft was the **Cessna** floatplane which carried wealthy businessmen from Long Island to New York (*bottom left*). The largest flying boat ever built – indeed, the biggest aeroplane in the world of its time – was the **Dornier Do X** which had no less than 12 engines!

The most advanced flying-boat yet built is the **Martin-P6M** Sea Master (*right*). Originally a mine-layer, it was turned into a successful passenger aircraft. (*Below right*) a **Canadair C1-215** used to carry water to fight forest fires.

PASSENGER AIR TRAVEL

After World War II, the **Dakotas** were used all over the world. Slowly, however, they were becoming out of date and a new and more powerful machine was needed. Lockheed in the USA had one answer, producing the **Constellation** with a cruising speed of just under 480 km/hr (300 mph). This was later to become the **Super Constellation.** In Britain, Vickers-Armstrong produced the Viking, an aircraft based on the wartime Wellington bomber. In 1949 the **Viscount** followed and 444 of these popular machines were built (*below*). It was the first successful turboprop airliner. There have been many versions of this machine, the latest, the **Super VC10,** completed in 1965, has seats for 174 passengers. Many of these are still in service around the world. In the same year, America brought out the **Boeing 377,** based on the successful **Superfortress** of World War II. It could carry 81 tourists or 50 first class passengers and had a lower-deck lounge. A later version of this, the **Boeing 747** (the 'Jumbo jet') is shown (*opposite top*).

Britain replied with the de Havilland pure-jet **Comet.** It had a cruising speed twice that of others, but was withdrawn after three terrible accidents. It was later replaced by **Comet 4** in 1958 when BOAC began the first jet service across the North Atlantic. In the same year Holland came into the picture with its **Fokker F-27 Friendship,** a twin-turboprop plane. Also in 1958 France introduced its twin-jet-engined **Caravelle.** This was the first aircraft to have its engines at the tail, an idea followed by the **VC10** shown (*opposite centre*). Another fine aircraft of this time was the **Hawker Siddeley Trident,** a 960 km/hr (600 mph) passenger plane. As jet engines became more efficient it was possible to use jets over short distances. One such was the American **Douglas DC-9,** a twin-engined jet, carrying up to 115 passengers.

A popular aircraft which appeared in 1972 is the Lockheed L-1011 **Tristar** shown (*opposite bottom*). Yet many people – if they have the money – prefer to travel by their own, private planes. One such, a Qantas de Havilland Canada Otter **Kerowagi** is shown (*below*).

A passenger plane takes off from somewhere in the world at least every five seconds, day and night, and there are more than 50 airliners over the Atlantic Ocean at the same time. This shows how air travel has become such a popular method of getting about. In the USA where long distances need to be covered, the railways have been nearly ruined by the growth of air travel.

One of the most important air-minded nations is the USSR which has a large fleet of civil aircraft. Her first important post-war aeroplane was the **Il-18**, then the **Tu-104** and in 1961 came the **Tu-114**, the heaviest commercial aircraft built up to that time. Another Russian plane – the **Ilyushin Il-63**

has a very long range and can easily fly from Moscow to New York non-stop and with 186 passengers.

Not all passenger aircraft are huge; many, mainly for the use of businessmen and diplomats, are quite small. Typical is the **Hawker Siddeley HS 125** business jet which can carry 6-12 passengers (*right*). Perhaps the most successful aeroplane built for the private owner was the **de Havilland Puss Moth,** a monoplane which first appeared in 1925. Today, most of these handy, private aeroplanes are American-built. The three main types in this field are the **Cessna, Piper** and **Beechcraft.** Many have been fitted with floats for fishing and similar pleasure trips.

THE FANTASTIC CONCORDE

Before 1976 a large number of big jet-planes such as the **Vickers VC-10** and the **Boeing 747** crossed the Atlantic at speeds of 960km/hr (600 mph) and over. But a new and sensational type of aircraft was needed, one that would be supersonic—that is, faster than the speed of sound. And that's about 335m (1100ft) per second! As the cost of such a machine would be enormous, Britain and France agreed to build it jointly. The result, of course, is the fantastic **Concorde.** Its first testing flight was March 1969 and on 21 January 1976, two supersonic Concordes took off at the same time, one from London to Bahrain, one from Paris to Rio de Janeiro. Both flights were successful – Concorde had been proved. It cruises some 17km (11 miles) above the earth at a speed of about 2110km/hr (1,320 mph) and that's twice the speed of a bullet! It cuts the world in half. When flying in the Concorde there is no sense of speed, with clouds far below. Although flights to New York were delayed because of fear of high noise levels on the ground, these now take place daily. The Soviet Union has built a very similar-looking machine. Known as the **Tu-144** it is slightly faster than the Anglo-French plane but carries fewer passengers.

MODERN MILITARY AIRCRAFT

Because many nations now have intercontinental missiles, the days of the large bomber are nearly over. Today is the day of the very fast (often three times the speed of sound) and powerfully-armed attack fighters. Almost all of today's military aircraft are jet-propelled and it is almost impossible to imagine a 'dogfight' of the future. Many post-war fighting planes took part in the Korean War of 1950-3, a proving ground for many bombers and fighters. The war did much to change the designs of the military aircraft of today. In this war an American **Allison J33** was the first victor in a jet-to-jet battle.

One of the world's largest bombers – the Boeing B-52H **Stratofortress** flies 1,055

km/hr (660 mph) at 6,100m (20,000ft) *(centre)*. The delta-winged Avro **Vulcan,** Britain's finest bomber *(below left).* Lockheed's C-5 **Galaxy** *(left),* a huge transport plane. The world's first Vertical/Short Take-Off and Landing plane (V/STOL), the **Harrier** *(bottom right).* Lockheed's F-104 **Starfighter,** the 'manned missile', flies at twice the speed of sound *(bottom far right).*

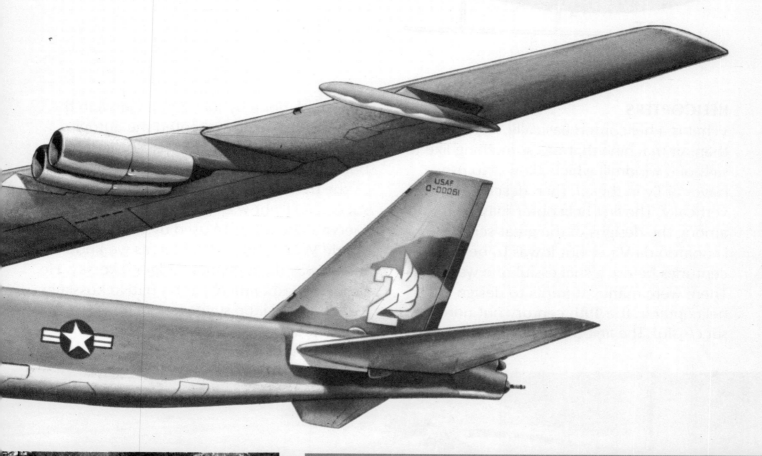

HELICOPTERS

What is a helicopter? Basically, it is a heavier-than-air machine that has something like the sails of a windmill which allow it to rise, hover or fly in the air, then descend vertically. The first helicopter may be found among the designs of the great scientist Leonardo da Vinci, but it was to be many centuries before a successful one was built. There were many attempts to design a helicopter in the 19th century but none were successful. The first that worked stemmed

from work done by Juan de la Cierva in the mid-1920s when he invented the autogiro, a machine similar to the modern helicopter, but with a standard propeller in front as well as the overhead rotors. Cierva's first successful flight was in 1923. A number of Cierva's aircraft were used by the RAF in World War II. The helicopter, as we know it today, was the invention of Igor Sikorsky. He began his experiments in his native Russia in 1909 but had little success until he emigrated to the USA. Unlike Cierva's

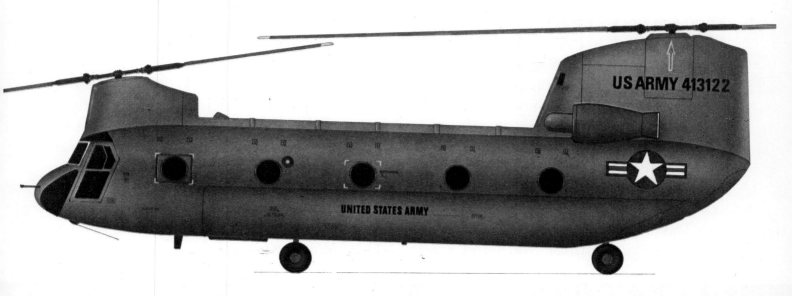

autogiros, his machines relied mainly on the overhead rotor blades and a small propeller set at the rear of the machine. Since then there have been many changes of design – twin blades, one blade and two side propellers, for example.

Sikorsky's first really successful helicopter was the **S-51** which was made by Westland of Britain. It was named **Dragonfly,** but since then improved versions have been the **Whirlwind, Wessex** and **Sea King.** These,

and other helicopters have been used by the military for transporting assault troops and wounded. They have also performed a number of civilian tasks such as rescuing people from the sea, burning buildings, mountains and many otherwise inaccessible places. They are also used for crop-spraying and seed-sowing, being much quicker than more traditional methods.

Helicopters are in many ways the most versatile aircraft in the world of aviation.

SPECIAL PURPOSE CRAFT

The helicopter, it has been said, can go anywhere, and do anything. Of all the special purpose aircraft it is unique. In recent years, however, there have been a number of aeroplanes and other craft which are used mainly for special tasks. One very important small job that aircraft have to do in Australia, South America and parts of Africa is to carry doctors to those needing urgent help. This is the well-known 'flying doctor' service. Also, in Australia, Northern Canada and Alaska there are the 'bush' pilots who help scattered villages keep in touch with the outside world. Canada also has a fleet of aircraft specially to fight forest fires. One is shown at work (*opposite*). Airsport has also grown enormously since World War II. Many light aeroplanes are now being made by Do-It-Yourself experts. The **Aerosport** (*below*) which is safe and easy to fly, is one. Gliding, hot-air ballooning and hang-gliding (see page 67) are all very popular today.

INTO ORBIT

12 April 1961 was a great day in history. That was the very first time that a manned craft had left the atmosphere of the earth to travel through outer space. That first man was a 37-year-old Russian cosmonaut, Yuri Gagarin. His craft was **Vostok 1,** in which he made an orbit of the earth. His flight time was 108 minutes. He was the first to prove that humans could survive blast-off, weightlessness and re-entry into the earth's atmophere. The launcher, which blasted him into space was kept secret by Russia for a while then a copy was publicly shown in 1967 (below).

The Soviet Union was definitely the leader in those early days of space travel. During 6-7 August 1961, another Russian cosmonaut, Gherman Titov, made 17 orbits and also became the first man whose flying time exceeded one day. (Two Americans, Alan Shepherd and later, Virgil Grissom, had made sub-orbital space voyages.) The first American actually to go into orbit was John Glenn on 20 February 1962 in the space capsule **Friendship 7.** A number of other space flights followed, but the next really important one was during March 1965 when, during its second orbit, one of the two-man Russian crew, Alexei Leonov actually left the craft **Voskhod 11** and walked in space. Later in 1965, in **Gemini 7,** Frank Borman and James Lovell remained in space for nearly two weeks. During this time they flew close to another American spacecraft, **Gemini 6,** manned by Wally Schirra and Tom Stafford.

A great number of American and Russian space flights followed and then . . . the great triumph! On 21 July 1969, Neil Armstrong, commander of **Apollo 11** and one of his two crewmates, Edwin Aldrin, actually stepped onto the surface of the moon. What a wonderful moment that must have been for the two daring Americans.

One of their typical astronaut's spacesuits is shown (opposite). (Far right above) are seen Edwin Aldrin climbing down **Eagle's** ladder; (centre) the two astronauts hoist their country's flag by the Sea of Tranquility and a notice which read: 'Here, men from planet Earth first set foot upon the Moon, July 1969 AD. We came in peace for all mankind.' Note how the flag hangs (bottom right). It has stiffened as there is no wind on the moon. However, those footprints will show visitors from another planet that someone got there first!

The experts are constantly thinking of, and planning for, the future. The space shuttle (*below*) will, it is hoped, make flights into orbit similar to the normal air travel of today. It takes off vertically then returns to land like an aeroplane.

That is yet to be – but what would those four famous brothers – the Montgolfiers and the Wrights – have even thought of such a suggestion?

ACKNOWLEDGMENTS

The publishers would like to thank the following individuals and organizations for their kind permission to reproduce the photographs in this book:

Air BP 81; All-Sport (Don Morley) 63 below right; American Museum in Great Britain (Cooper-Bridgeman) 20-21; J P Anazel 14; Anderson 43 below, 46 above left; Associated Press 67 above; Beken of Cowes 32 above, 32-33; Boeing Company 75 above; British Rail 46 above right and below; British Tourist Authority 35; Canadian Pacific 39 above; C.C.Q. (N Shepherd) 44 below; J A Coiley 45 below; Cooper-Bridgeman 7, 24-25, 34 below, 37 above; Crown Copyright, HMSO 27 below; Daily Telegraph (Mike Sheil) 65 right; Deutsches Bundesbahn 47 above; Ron Dorman 33 above right; H Dougall 74; F. Dumbleton 37 below; Mary Evans Picture Library 19 below, 64, 66; Ford Motor Co. 56-57; C J Gammell 38 above and below, 40 above, 41 below left; General Motors 56; J Gilbert 70 below, 82 below; Glenn-Martin CO. 83 above; V Goldberg 36 below; V Hand 28-29, 38-39, 41 above, 47 below; Hawker Siddeley Aviation Ltd. 4-5; Jan Heese 62-63, 63 above; M Holford 15; Imperial War Museum 72-73; A F Kersting 16; C & B Leimbach 33 above left; Lockheed Aircraft Corp. 85 below; London Art Technical Drawings Ltd. 58 above, 59 above and below; London Transport 45 above; Mansell Collection 6; Mariners' Museum, Newport News, Va. 20 above; Merseyside County Museum, Dept. of Maritime History (Paul Forrester) 19 above; Murray 43 above right; NASA 95 left, above right, centre right and below right; National Maritime Museum 24 below, (M Holford) 17, 22-23 above; National Motor Museum 53 above, 54-55 below; New Zealand Railways 41 below right; The Parker Gallery 18; Picturepoint Ltd. 13; Pilatus Railway 42 below; P & O 31 below; Popperfoto Ltd. 12 above and below; F L Pugh 40 below 42 above; Qantas Airways Ltd. 85 above; Radio Times Hulton Picture Library 9, 44 above; Peter Roberts Collection 8, 48, 48-49, 50, 51 above and below, 52, 53 below, 54-55 above, 55 above, 58 below, 60-61; Ronan Picture Library 68; The Director, The Science Museum 21 above, 24 above, 27 above, 34 above; Shell 31 above; K Sissons 82 above; Spectrum Colour Library 22-23 below, 65 left, 69, 76 above, 77 above, 88 above and below, 94 left and right; Tony Stone Associates 67 below; J Stroud 84 above; J W R Taylor 75 below, 78-79, 82-83 below, 84 below, 85 centre, 86-87, 87 below, 89 left and right, 90, 92, 93; PN Trotter 43 above left; George Allen & Unwin from "The Ra Expeditions" by Thor Heyerdahl 10-11; Westland Aircraft Ltd. 91; ZEFA 62 above.

First published in 1978 by Octopus Books Limited 59 Grosvenor Street London W1

ISBN 0 7064 0793 8

© 1978 Octopus Books Limited

Produced by Mandarin Publishers Limited, Westlands Road, Quarry Bay, Hong Kong

Printed in Singapore